Contents

Welcome to Rise and Shine Towers

1 Trace and match.

Hi! I'm Dexter.

My name's Mia.

I'm Bruno.

My name's Elena.

2 🖍️ 💬 Trace and colour. Then ask and answer.

Tell me!
How old are you?
I'm 4.

What's your favourite colour? Tell a friend.

Extra time?

3 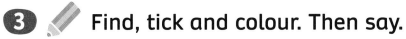 Find, tick and colour. Then say.

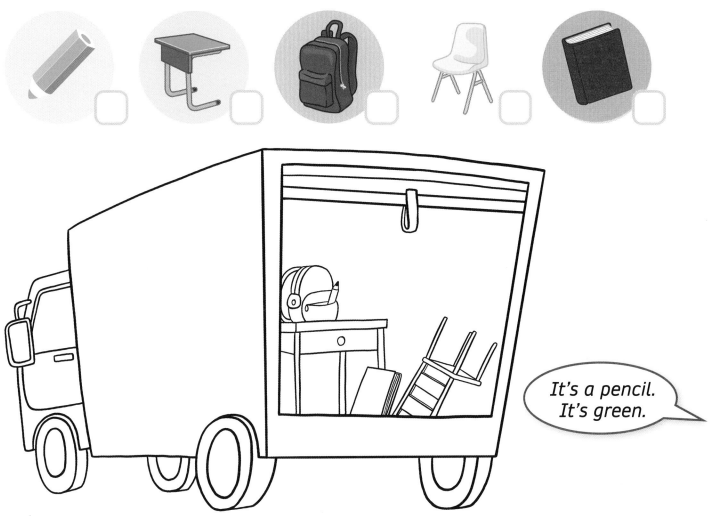

It's a pencil.
It's green.

4 Draw and write for you. Then say.

Hi! My name is
_____.

I'm _____.

colour me

Write the numbers: 1 ___ 3 4 5 ___ 8 9 ___

Extra time?

3

Old toys, new toys

Let's review! PB p6 Find and colour. Then trace and say.

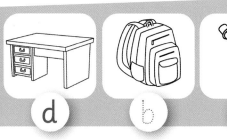

d   b   p

1 Trace and match.

ball

train

robot

teddy bear

car

doll

elephant

tablet

Tell me!

Look at my new words. Match and colour.

a

Toys

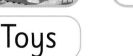

b

School things

Say the words in alphabetical order.

Extra time?

1 🎧 1.06 **Listen and circle.**

1 ⓐ 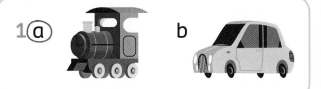 b

2 a b

3 a b

4 a b

2 **Read and tick (✓) or cross (✗).**

1 It's a teddy bear. ✗

2 It's a robot.

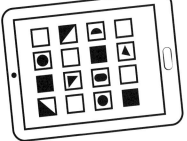

3 It's a tablet.

4 It's a car.

I can shine!

3 🖍 **Colour a toy in Activity 2. Write. Then tell a friend.**

It's a _____.

colour me

Write your favourite toy word. _____

Extra time?

⑤

1 PB p12–13 ➡ **Which toy is new? Look and tick (✓).**

① ② ③ ④

2 🖊 **Find and colour. Then circle.**

Let's imagine!

It's a doll /
an elephant.

I can shine! ✳✳

3 🖊 **Draw. Then say.**

And you? What's your favourite toy at school?

colour me

Rate the story and tell a friend. ☆☆☆

Extra time?

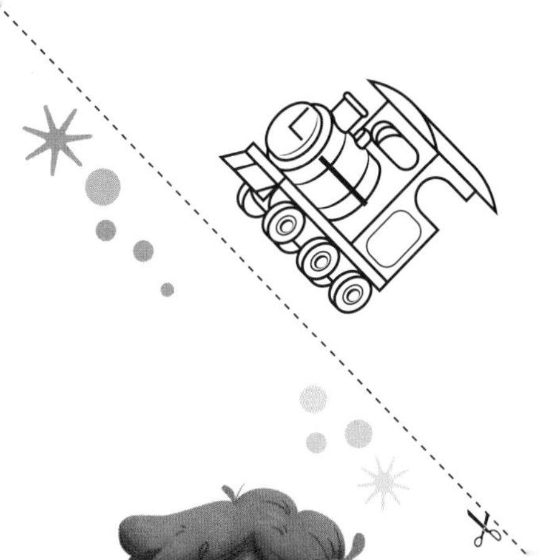

Lesson 4 ➡ Vocabulary and structures

1 Read and trace. Then circle.

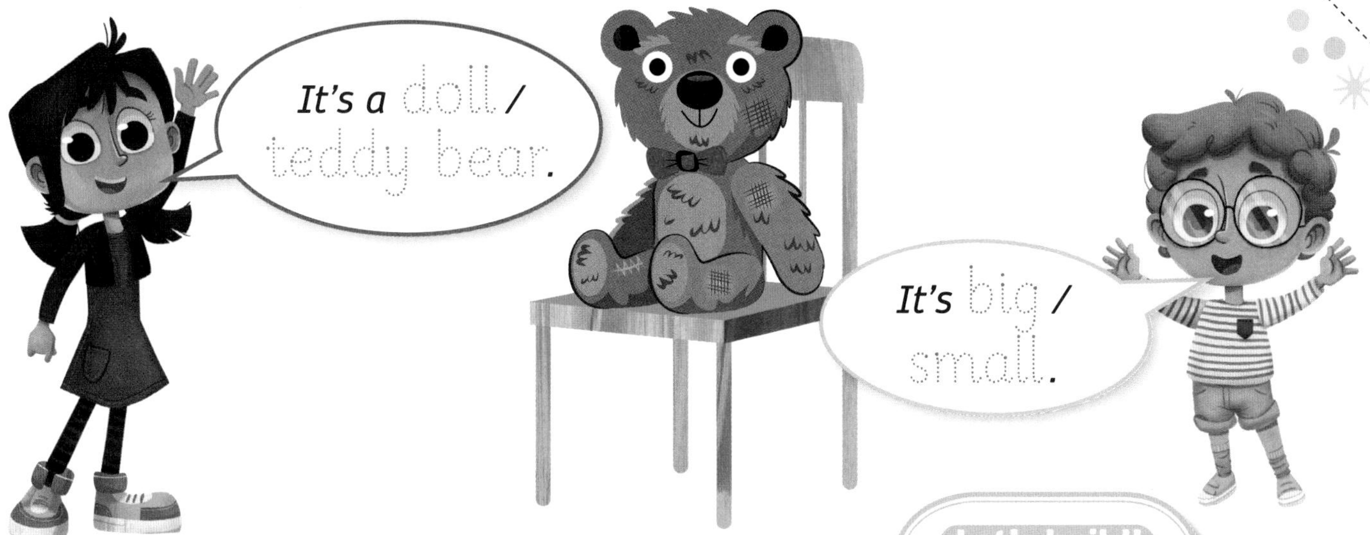
It's a doll / teddy bear.
It's big / small.

2 Follow, find and number. Then say.

Let's build!

What is it?

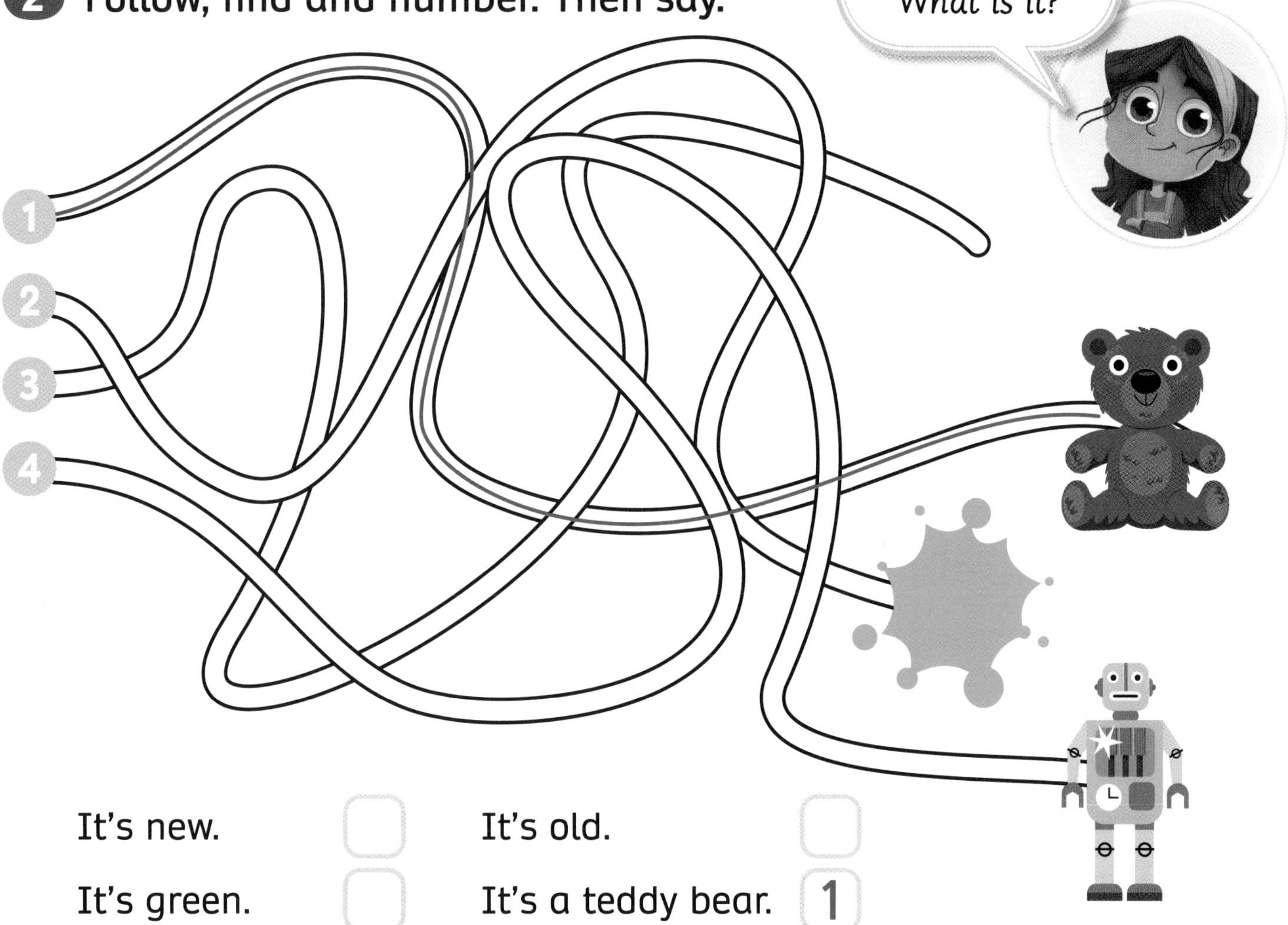
1
2
3
4

It's new.		It's old.	
It's green.		It's a teddy bear.	1

Think of an old toy you've got. Draw and tell a friend. **Extra time?**

1 🎧 1.13 ✏️ Listen and colour.

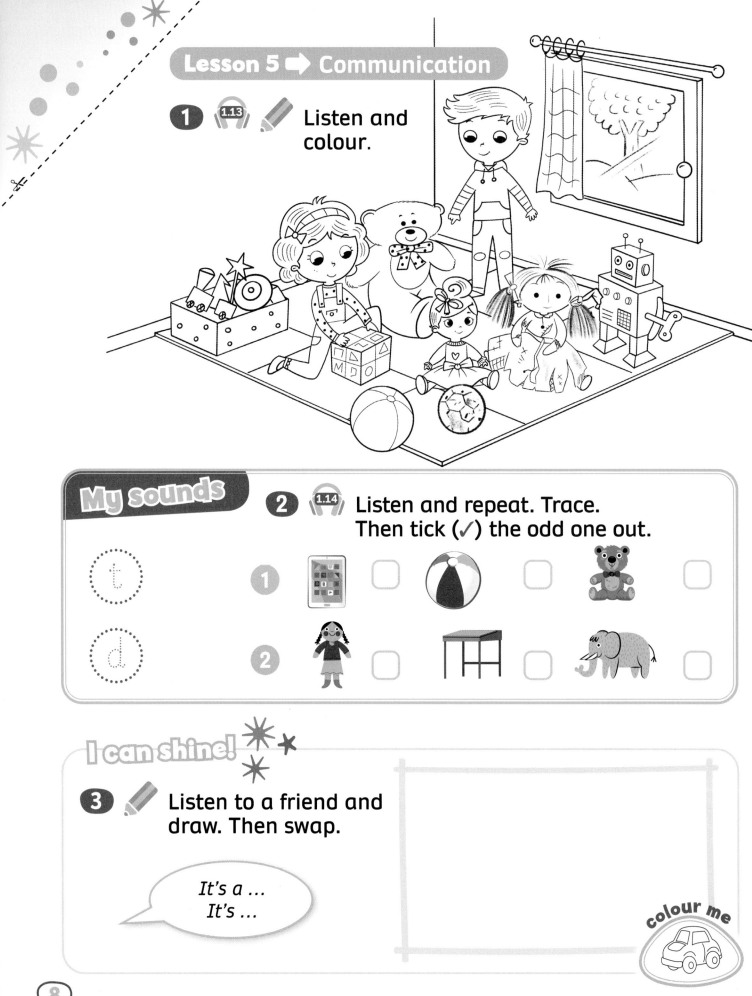

My sounds

2 🎧 1.14 Listen and repeat. Trace. Then tick (✓) the odd one out.

t

d

1

2

I can shine! ✳️✳️

3 ✏️ Listen to a friend and draw. Then swap.

It's a …
It's …

colour me

1 Circle the odd one out. Then say.

It's a new doll.

1 New

2 Old

I can shine!

2 Look and write. Then act out.

Think and share
Do you share your toys?

What's this?

It's a _____.

colour me

What toys do your friends share with you? Talk with a friend.

1 Trace and number.

It's …

a ball. ☐   a tablet. ☐

a car. ☐   a doll. ☐

a teddy bear. ☐   a robot. ☐

a train. ☐   an elephant. 1

| 1 | 2 | 3 | 4 | 5 | 6 | 7 | 8 |

2 Choose and tick (✓). Draw and colour. Then tell a friend.

It's …

new. ☐   small. ☐

old. ☐   big. ☐

It's …

green. ☐   yellow. ☐

blue. ☐   red. ☐

It's a big car.
It's red.

What's this? It's a __ __ __ __ box.

Extra time?

3 Stick, draw and colour.
Then play the game.

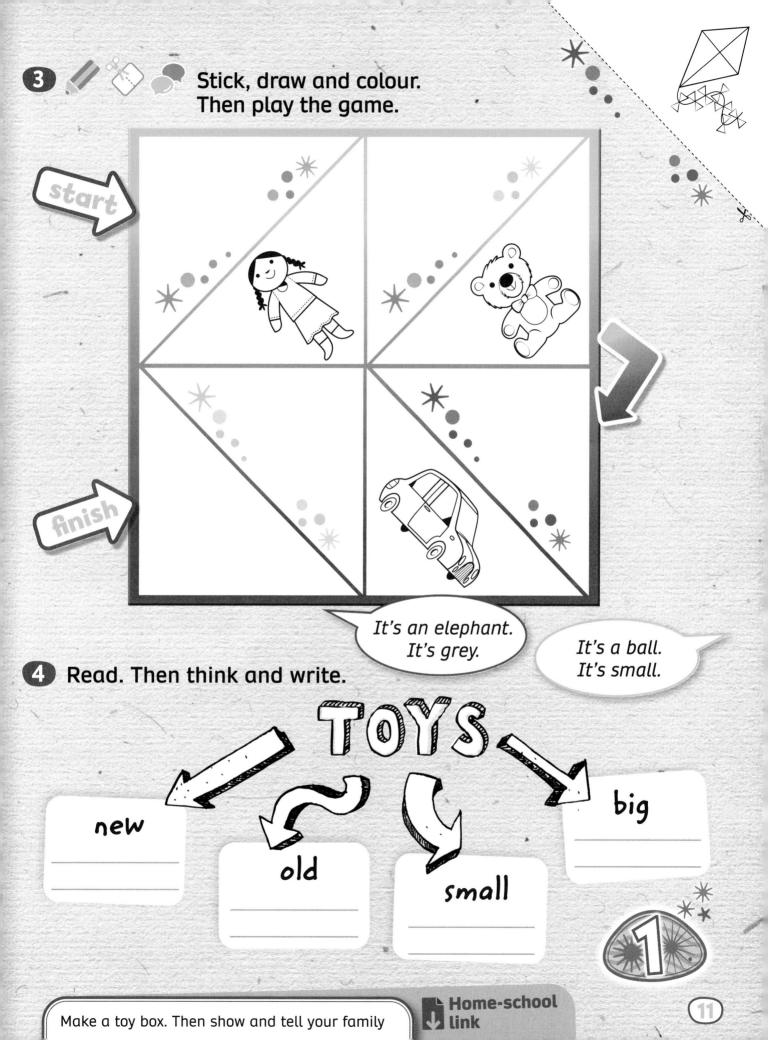

start

finish

It's an elephant.
It's grey.

It's a ball.
It's small.

4 Read. Then think and write.

TOYS

new

old

small

big

Make a toy box. Then show and tell your family

Home-school
link

2 All kinds of families

Let's review! PB p10–11 ➡ Find and trace. Then say.

b t c

1 Trace and match.

brother

sister

mum

dad

granny

grandad

auntie

uncle

Tell me!
Look at my new words. Match and colour.

Toys

Family

Say the words in alphabetical order.

Extra time?

1 🎧 2.06 **Listen and match.**

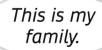
This is my family.

①    ②    ③    ④

a    b    c    d

2 **Read. Then look at Activity 1 and number.**

This is my granny, my grandad and my sister. ☐

This is my mum, my dad and my brother. ☐

I can shine!

3 ✏️ **Draw someone in your family. Write. Then tell a friend.**

This is my _____.

colour me

Write your favourite family word. _____

Extra time?

13

1 `PB p22–23` ➡ **Who is in Bruno's family? Look and tick (✓).**

 1

 2

 3

2 **Follow. Then circle.**

Let's imagine!

I've got a brother / an auntie.

I can shine!

3 🖍 **Draw.**
Then say.

And you?
Who's in your
family?

colour me

Rate the story and tell a friend. ☆☆☆

Extra time?

1 **Read and trace. Then circle.**

1 *I've got a* dog / bird.

2 *I've got a* cat / bird.

3 *I've got a* fish / cat.

2 **Match and say.**

1  **2**  **3**  **4**

Let's build!

I've got a brother.

a  **b**  **c**  **d**

I've got a sister.   I've got a granny.   I've got a cat.   I've got a mum.

Think of a pet for you. Draw and tell a friend.

Extra time?

15

1 🎧 2.13 Listen and number.

 a

 b

 c

 d **1**

My sounds

2 🎧 2.14 Listen and repeat. Trace. Then match.

I can shine!

3 💬 Tick (✓) for you. Then tell a friend.

*I've got a ...
And you?*

colour me

1 Read and match. Then say.

This is for my cousin.

1 **2** **3** **4**

a neighbour **b** cousin **c** friend **d** pet

I can shine!

Think and share

Do you help your friends and family?

2 Draw and write. Then act out.

This is for my _____ .

Who do you help in your family? Tell a friend.

Extra time?

1 Trace. Then number for Dexter.

Bruno is my brother.

This is my ...

mum. [1] granny. ☐ auntie. ☐

dad. ☐ grandad. ☐ uncle. ☐ sister. ☐

 1  2  3  4  5  6  7

2 💬 Look and read. Tick (✓) or cross (✗) for you. Then tell a friend.

I've got a bird and a cat.

I've got a dog and a fish.

	🐦	🐱	🐕	🐟
1	✓	✓	✗	✗
2	✗	✗	✓	✓
3 Me				

18

Who's this? It's ___ ___ ___ ___ ___ ___ Felipe.

Extra time?

3 ✏️ 💬 Stick, draw and colour. Then complete the family tree.

This is my grandad.

I've got a dog.

pet

4 Read. Then think and write.

Me

Family

Friends

Pets

Make a picture album page. Then show and tell your family

Review 1 Important to me

1 ✏️ Colour and say.

It's a train.

2 🎧 2.19 💬 Listen and number. Then ask and answer.

a   b   c   d   e

1

Who's this?

This is my ...

What's this?

It's a ...

3 Join the dots. Then read, trace and circle.

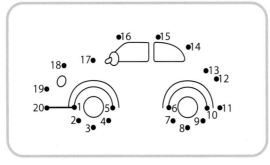

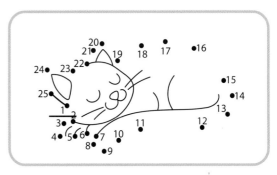

1 It's a train / car.

2 This is my cat / dog.

4 Read and trace. Then tick (✓) for you.

I've got …

a new bike.   an old plane.   a big dog.   a small fish.

5 Think of a toy to play with. Draw, write and say.

Let's play with the _____.

Mini-project

6 Think of a toy to give to your best friend. Draw and write.

This is for you,

_____.

It's a _____.

Time to shine!

7 Read and colour.

1 I can write toy words.   ✓ ? ✗

2 I can write family words.   ✓ ? ✗

3 I can talk about things and people important to me.   ✓ ? ✗

4 I completed Review 1!   ✓ ? ✗

3 Amazing bodies

Let's review! `PB p20–21` ➡ Find and trace. Then say.

a u g

1 Trace and match.

eyes arms

nose legs

mouth hands

ears feet

Tell me!
Look at my new words. Match and colour.

a

The body

b

School things

Say the words in alphabetical order.

Extra Time?

1 🎧 ³·⁰⁶ Listen and tick (✓).

2 Read and count. Then write.

My body

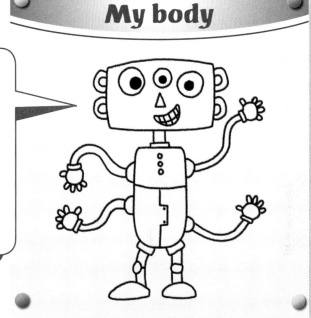

I've got ___2___ legs.
I've got _____ arms.
I've got _____ eyes.
I've got _____ ears.

3 ✏ Draw your robot. Write. Then tell a friend.

I've got _____
_____
_____ .

colour me

Write your favourite body word. _____

Extra Time?

1 PB p34–35 ➡ **Which is the odd one out? Look and tick (✓).**

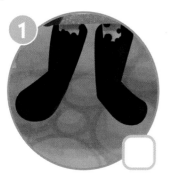 1

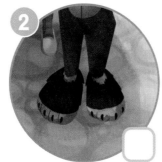 2

 3

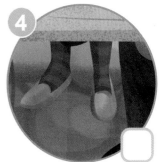 4

2 ✏ **Find and colour. Then circle.**

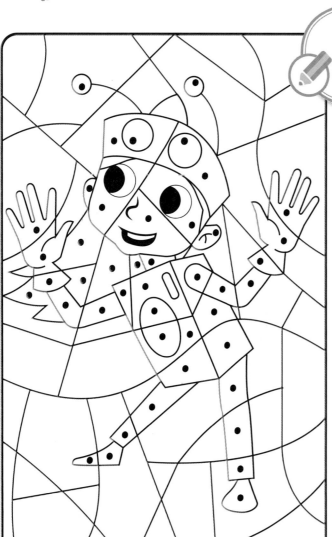

Let's imagine!

My auntie / granny / friend can dance.

I can shine!

3 ✏ **Draw. Then say.**

And you? Can you dance?

colour me

Rate the story and tell a friend. ☆☆☆

Extra Time?

1 Trace. Then read and circle.

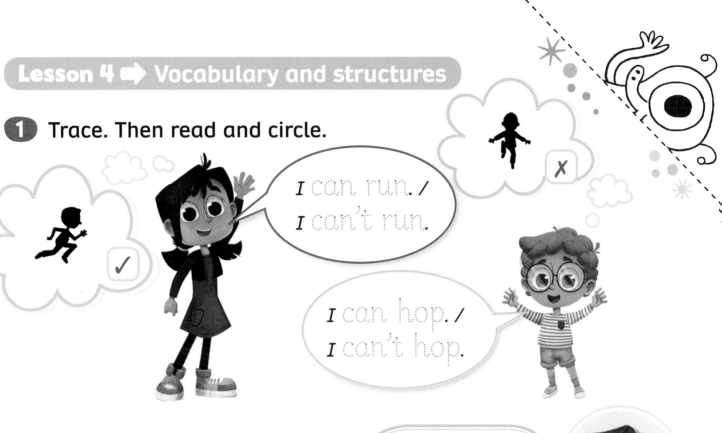

I can run. /
I can't run.

I can hop. /
I can't hop.

2 Look, read and write.

Let's build!

What can you see?

1 I can hop. `c`

2 I can jump.

3 I can dance.

4 I can run.

Think of something you can do. Draw and tell a friend.

Extra Time?

1 🎧 3.13 Listen and tick (✓) or cross (✗).

	run	jump	hop	dance
1	✓			
2				

My sounds

2 🎧 3.14 Listen and repeat. Trace. Then match.

m
n

I can shine!

3 What can you do? Circle. Then tell a friend.

I *can / can't* jump.

I *can / can't* dance.

I *can / can't* run.

I *can / can't* hop.

colour me

1 Look, read and number. Then say.

touch your nose ☐

don't move ☐

close your eyes ☐

clap your hands 1

1 – Clap your hands!

Think and share

Do you play together with friends? What games?

I can shine!

2 Trace and write. Then act out.

Close your eyes.
Well done!

_____ your _____.
Well done!

_____ your _____.
Well done!

colour me

Play a clapping game with a friend.

Extra Time?

27

1 Draw and trace. Then colour.

I've got ...

1 mouth.   4 arms.
1 nose.   4 hands.
3 eyes.   3 legs.
6 ears.   3 feet.

2 Match and trace. Then play with a friend.

1

I can dance.

I can run.

I can hop.

I can jump.

2

3

4

I can run.

Elephant.

I've got big feet. I'm a dog. I can't _____ _____ _____ _____ in the story. Who am I? Look at PB p 34-35.

Extra Time?

3 Stick and put a tick (✓) or a cross (✗). Then tell a friend.

I've got 2 noses and 4 feet.

I can't jump.

4 Think and write for you. Then tell a friend and write.

		Me	
I can	✓		
I can't	✗		

Make an 'I can do it!' poster. Then show and tell your family

 Home-school link

29

4 Let's eat up

Let's review! PB p32–33 → Find and write. Then say.

h

1 Trace and match.

bread

milk

chicken

cheese

olives

tomatoes

bananas

strawberries

Tell me! Look at my new words. Match and colour.

a

The body

b

Food

30

Say the words in alphabetical order.

Extra time?

1 Listen and tick (✓) or cross (✗).

2 🖍 Trace. Then read and draw ☺ or ☹.

I like *bananas.*

I like *bread.*

I don't like *tomatoes.*

I don't like *chicken.*

I can shine!

3 🖍 Colour the food you like in Activity 2. Write. Then tell a friend.

I like _____.

colour me

Write your favourite food word. _____

Extra time?

31

1 PB p44–45 **Look and find. Then tick (✓) the food you see together.**

1  +  ☐ **2**  +  ☐

3  +  ☐

Let's imagine!
I like cheese and strawberries.

2 🖊 **Read and find. Then colour.**

I can shine!

3 🖊 **Draw. Then say.**

And you? What's your favourite food at school?

colour me

Rate the story and tell a friend. ☆☆☆   **Extra time?**

1 Trace. Then look and write.

1 [d] I like sandwiches.   2 [ ] I like pizza.

3 [ ] I don't like milkshake.   4 [ ] I don't like ice cream.

2 Follow and find. Trace and circle for Elena. Then say.

Let's build!

Ask me questions about food!

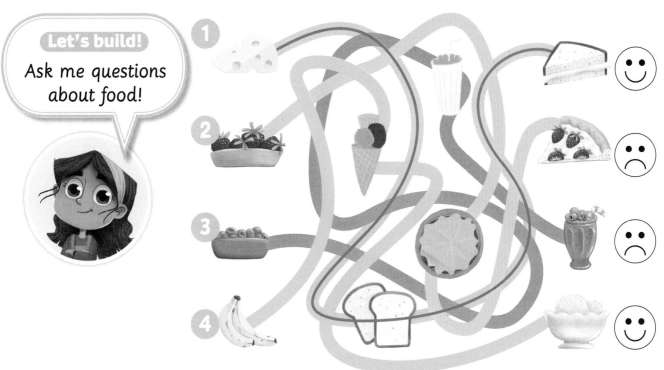

1 Do you like cheese sandwiches?   2 Do you like strawberry pizza?
Yes, I do. / No, I don't.   Yes, I do. / No, I don't.

3 Do you like olive milkshake?   4 Do you like banana ice cream?
Yes, I do. / No, I don't.   Yes, I do. / No, I don't.

Think of your favourite sandwich. Draw and tell a friend.

Extra time?

1 🎧 4.13 Listen and tick (✓) or cross (✗).

 **My sounds**

2 🎧 4.14 ✏️ Listen and repeat. Trace. Then colour 'ch' words blue and 'h' words red.

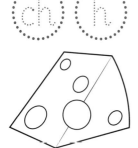   

I can shine!

3 ✏️ Circle the food you like. Ask and answer. Then draw for a friend.

My food

bread	milkshake
tomatoes	sandwiches
pizza	cheese
strawberries	ice cream

My friend's food

Do you like bread?

Yes, I do.

colour me

1 Circle four differences. Then say.

1

2

Picture 1. Pasta.

Think and share

Think about when you order food. Do you say 'please'?

I can shine!

2 Read and choose three foods. Write. Then act out.

Menu

milkshake
strawberries
pizza
pasta
rice
salad
soup
sandwiches
ice cream

Can I have some ..., please?

colour me

Guess your friend's favourite food.

Extra time?

1 🖍 Read and draw.

I like cheese and olives. I don't like tomatoes and bananas.

I like milk and chicken. I don't like strawberries and bread.

2 💬 Trace and match to make your own food. Then ask and answer.

Menu

1 cheese   ice cream

2 olive   milkshake

3 banana   sandwiches

4 strawberry   pizza

Do you like …?

Yes, I do. / No, I don't.

What's this? i _ _ _   c _ _ _ _ _

Extra time?

3 ✏️ ✂️ 💬 **Stick, draw and colour. Then play the game.**

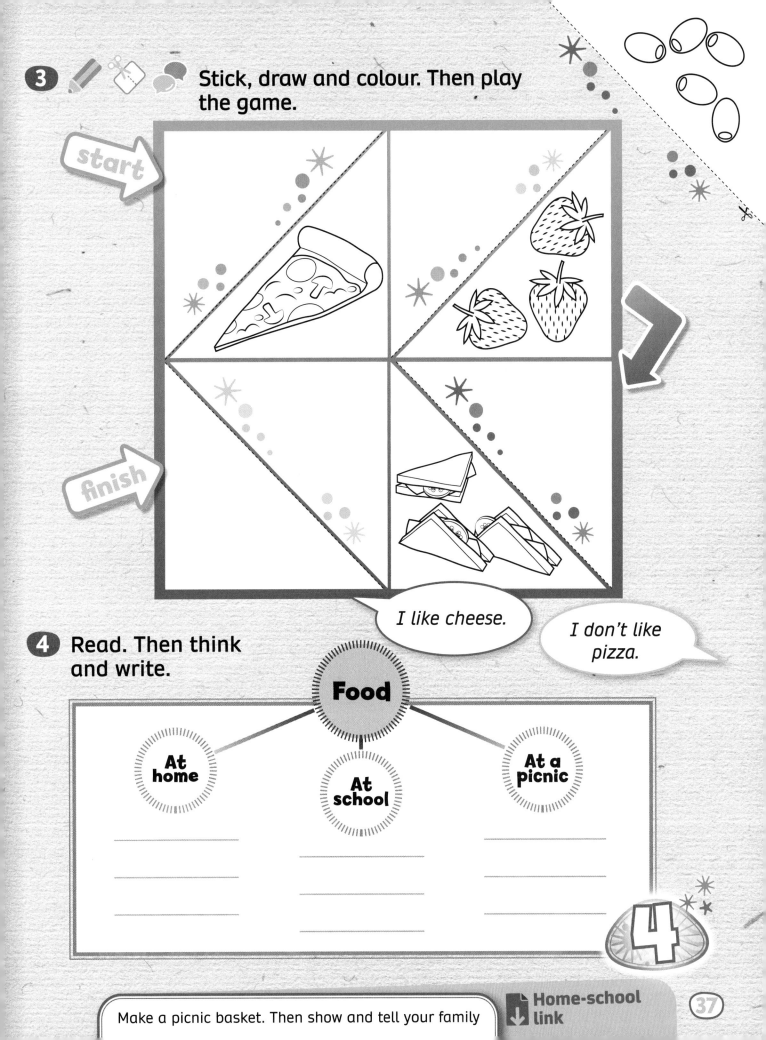

start

finish

I like cheese.

I don't like pizza.

4 **Read. Then think and write.**

Food

At home

At school

At a picnic

Make a picnic basket. Then show and tell your family

Home-school link

Review 2 All about me

1 (4.19) Listen and follow. Then tick (✓).

2 Trace. Then look at Activity 1 and match.

1 *I like* bananas. *I like* strawberries. *I don't like* milk.

2 *I don't like* bananas. *I don't like* tomatoes. *I like* chicken.

3 Ask and answer.

Do you like olives?

Yes, I do.

Do you like cheese?

No, I don't.

4 Look and tick (✓) for you. Then act out.

MENU

Can I have some pizza, please?

5 Trace. Then look and match.

1

FACT FILE

I've got 4 legs *and 2 big ears. I can* run.

2

FACT FILE

I've got small eyes. *I can* hop.

Mini-project

6 Think of a pet for you. What can your pet do? Draw and write.

I've got _____ and _____ . I can _____ .

Time to shine!

7 Read and colour.

1 I can write body words.    ✓ ? ✗

2 I can write food words.   ✓ ? ✗

3 I can talk about what I like and have got.   ✓ ? ✗

4 I completed Review 2!    ✓ ? ✗

5 Nature around us

Let's review! PB p42-43 ➡ Find and write. Then say.

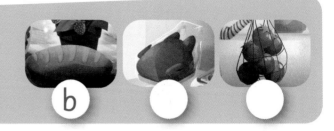

b

1 Look and write.

| frog | lizard | mouse | turtle | fox | ~~owl~~ | rabbit | duck |

1
2
3
4
5
6
7
8

___owl___

Tell me!
Look at my new words. Match and colour.

a

Toys

b

Nature

Say the words in alphabetical order.

Extra time?

1 🎧 5.06 Listen and tick (✓) or cross (✗).

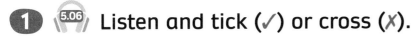

① ② ③ ④

✓ ☐ ☐ ☐

2 Trace. Then count and write.

I can see __6__ frogs, _____ rabbits, _____ owls and _____ lizards.

I can shine! ✳

3 ✏ Draw and write.
Then tell a friend.

I can see
_____.

colour me

Write your favourite animal word. _____

1 PB p 56–57 ➡ **Circle the odd one out.**

①  ②  ③  ④

2 **Join the dots. Then read and circle.**

Let's imagine!
I can see an owl /
a butterfly.

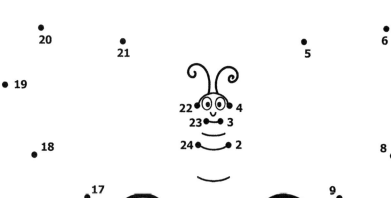

• 20
• 21
• 19
• 5
• 6
22 • 4
23 • 3
• 7
24 • 2
• 18
• 8
• 17
• 9
16 •
25 • 1
• 10
• 13
15 •
14 •
12 •
• 11

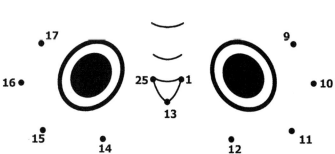

I can shine!

3 ✏️ **Draw. Then say.**

And you? Can you
see a big animal?

colour me

Rate the story and tell a friend. ☆☆☆

**Extra
time?**

1 Trace. Then read and circle.

1 Is it a ladybird?   Yes, it is / No, it isn't.

2 Is it a bee?   Yes, it is. / No, it isn't.

2 Follow and find. Then write.

Let's build!
Which animals are in the park?

butterfly ~~ant~~ ladybird bee

1 It's a small ___ant___.

2 It's a red _____.

3 It's a big _____.

4 It's a blue _____.

Think of your favourite small animal. Draw and tell a friend.

Extra time?

43

1 🎧 5.13 Listen and number.

My sounds

2 🎧 5.14 Listen and repeat. Trace.
Then tick (✓) the odd one out.

I can shine!

3 💬 ✏️ Ask and answer with a friend.
Then draw.

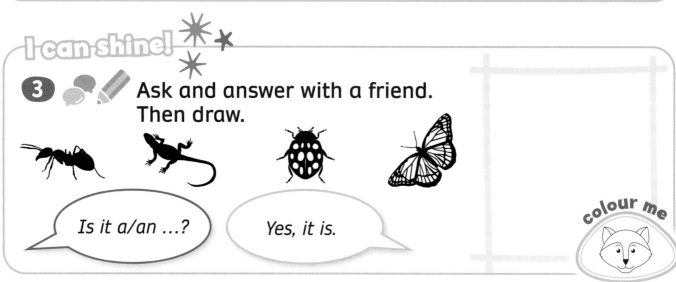

Is it a/an ...?

Yes, it is.

colour me

1 Read and trace. Tick (✓) or cross (✗). Then say.

> Look at the frog.

pond ✓

flowers

tree

grass

Think and share

Think about a park near you. Can you find a pond with ducks or frogs?

I can shine!

2 Choose an animal home and draw an animal in it. Write. Then act out.

- pond
- tree
- grass
- flowers

> Look at the _____.
> Let's find a _____!

colour me

What can you see in your classroom? Tell a friend.

Extra time?

1 **Look. Then count and write.**

frogs   lizards   ~~mouse~~   turtles   foxes   owls   rabbits   ducks

I can see 1 __mouse__ , 2 _____ , 3 _____ , 4 _____ ,

5 _____ , 6 _____ , 7 _____ and 8 _____ .

2 🖉 💬 **Trace and circle. Draw and write. Then ask and answer.**

Fact File 1

Is it a bee?

No, it isn't.

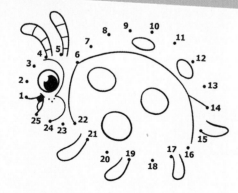

FACT FILE 2

It's a ladybird / butterfly.

It's a _____ .

What can you see? I can see a
_____ _____ .

Extra time?

3 ✏️ ✂️ 💬 **Stick and colour. Then tell a friend.**

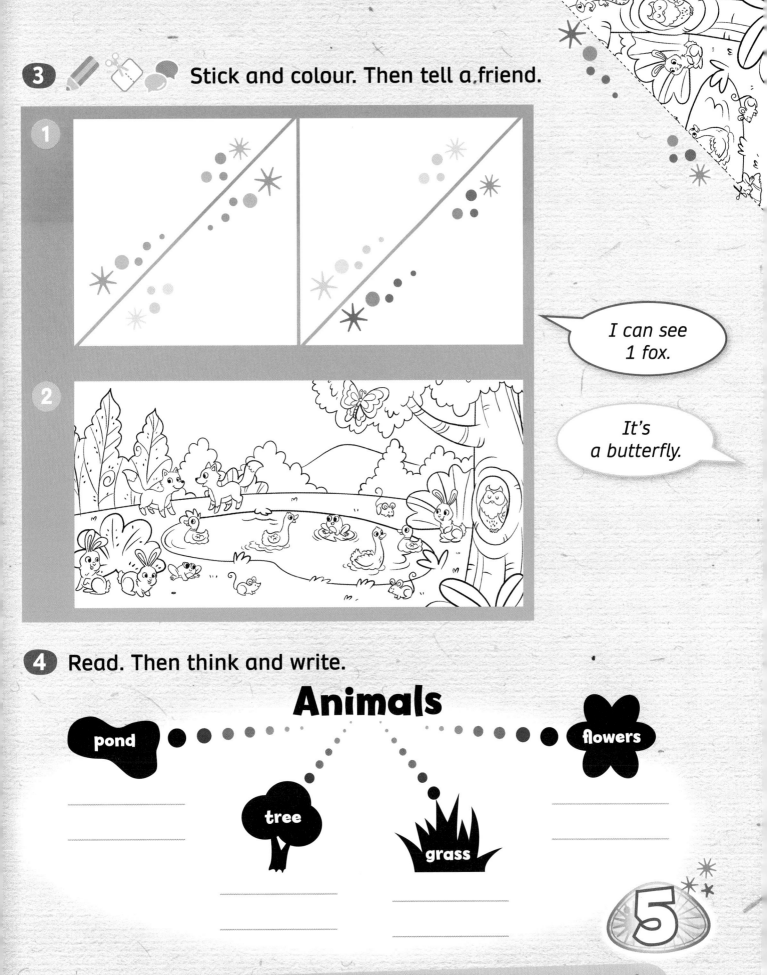

1

I can see 1 fox.

2

It's a butterfly.

4 **Read. Then think and write.**

Animals

pond

flowers

tree

grass

_____
_____

_____
_____

5

Make an origami owl. Then show and tell your family

6 Let's dress up

Let's review! PB p54–55 Find and write. Then say.

d

1 Look and write.

shirt   trousers   jumper   shoes   dress   shorts   T-shirt   ~~pyjamas~~

pyjamas

Tell me! Look at my new words. Match and colour.

Clothes

Nature

Say the words in alphabetical order.   Extra time?

1 🎧 6.06 ✏️ Listen and colour.

2 Look at Activity 1. Then read and write.

shoes ~~shorts~~ trousers shirt

1 I'm wearing purple shorts____.

2 I'm wearing black _____.

3 I'm wearing pink _____.

4 I'm wearing a blue _____.

I can shine!

3 Tick (✓) and say. Then tell a friend.

I'm wearing ...

pyjamas ☐
a T-shirt ☐   a dress ☐
shoes ☐
trousers ☐
a jumper ☐

colour me

Write your favourite clothes word. _____

Lesson 3 ➡ Story

1 PB p66-67 ➡ **Who is happy? Look and circle.**

①  **②**  **③**

2 🖍 Find and colour. Then say.

Let's imagine!
I'm wearing a purple jumper / T-shirt, black shoes and blue trousers / shorts.

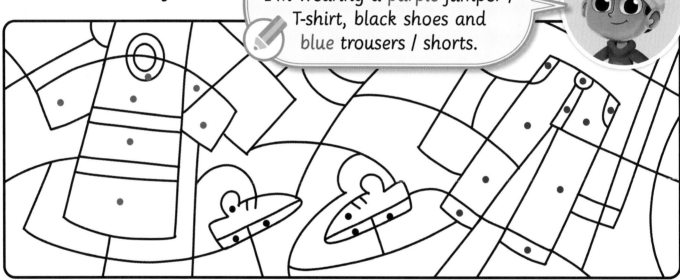

I can shine!

3 🖍 Draw and colour. Write for you. Then say.

I'm wearing
_____.

colour me

Rate the story and tell a friend. ☆☆☆

Extra time?

1 **Trace. Then read and number.**

1 I'm hot.

2 I'm happy.

3 I'm sad.

4 I'm cold.

2 **Read and write.**

Let's build!
What are you wearing?

| ~~cold~~ hot sad happy |

1 I'm wearing pyjamas. I'm _____ cold _____.

2 I'm wearing my favourite dress. I'm _____.

3 I'm wearing two jumpers. I'm _____.

4 I'm wearing a yellow T-shirt. I don't like yellow. I'm _____. But I've got a red jumper. I like red!

Think of your favourite clothes. Draw and tell a friend.

Extra time?

1 🎧 6.13 Listen and tick (✓).

My sounds

2 🎧 0.00 Listen and repeat. Trace. Then colour 'j' words blue and 'sh' words green.

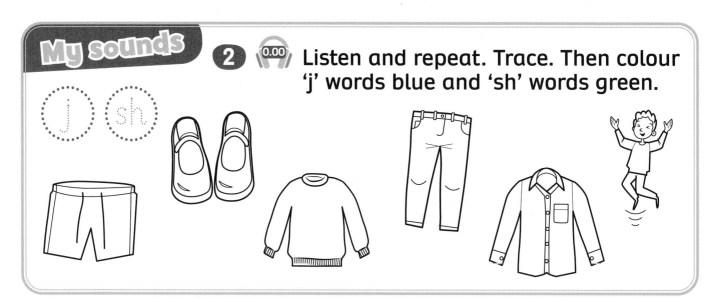

I can shine!

3 ✏️ Colour clothes for a cold day. Write. Then tell a friend.

I'm wearing

_____

and _____.

colour me

1 **Look and write. Then say.**

boots   skirt   hat   ~~jeans~~

1   **2**   **3**   **4**

<u>jeans</u>   _____   _____   _____

I'm wearing jeans.

Think and share

Think about a festival. Do you dress up with your friends?

I can shine!

2 🖍 **Draw special clothes for your friend. Write. Then act out.**

Wear _____ and _____!

colour me

What are your favourite special clothes? Tell a friend.

Extra time?

trousers   shorts
a shirt   a T-shirt
shoes   pyjamas
a dress   a jumper

1 Trace and write.

I'm wearing
a T-shirt,
_____
and
_____.

I'm wearing
_____,
_____
and
_____.

2 Trace and match. Then act out.

I'm sad.

I'm hot.

 1

 2

 3

 4

I'm cold.

I'm happy.

54

What's this? It's a ___ ___.

Extra time?

3 🖊 ✂️ 💬 **Stick, draw and colour. Then play the game.**

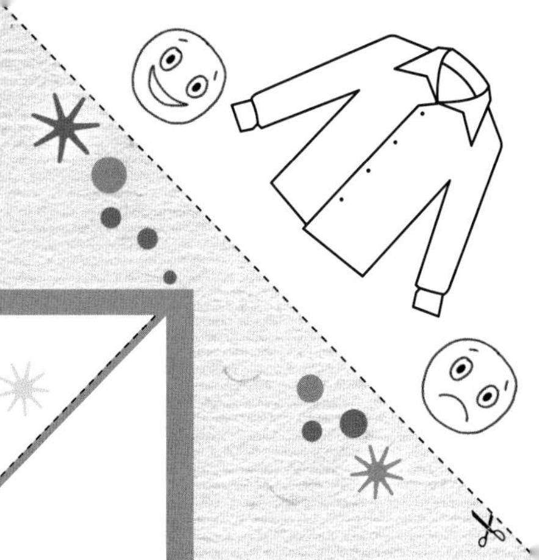

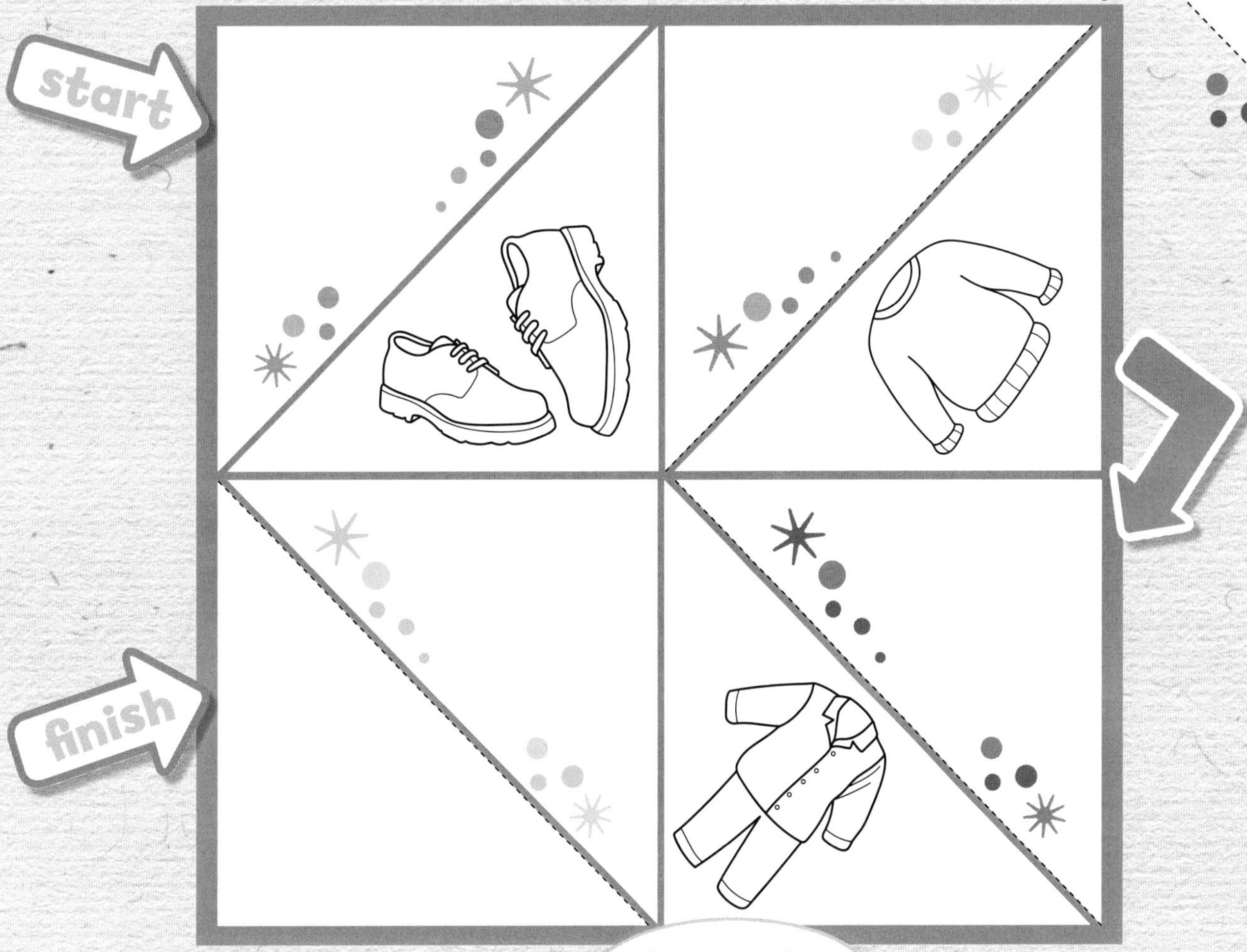

start

finish

I'm wearing pyjamas.

I'm wearing a hat. I'm hot.

4 **Read. Then think and write.**

My Clothes

(**Favourite**)   (**Special**)

Make a party hat. Then show and tell your family.

Home-school link

Review 3 Around me

1 Find and circle 5 differences. **2** 🎧 6.19 Listen and tick (✓).

3 Look at Activity 1. Trace. Then read and number.

I'm wearing shorts.
I can see a mouse.

I'm wearing a dress.
I can see a lizard.

4 💬 Play *Which picture?* with a friend.

I'm wearing jeans.
I can see a frog.

Is it Picture 2?

Yes, it is.

5 **Trace. Then look and write.** sad hot happy

1

I'm wearing pyjamas.
I'm _____.

2

I'm wearing trousers and a jumper.
I'm _____.

3

I'm wearing a shirt.
I'm _____.

Mini-project

6 Draw clothes for your friend's dress-up party. Then write and say.

I'm wearing _____.
I'm _____.

Time to shine!

7 **Read and colour.**

1 I can write animal words.  ✓ ? ✗

2 I can write clothes words.  ✓ ? ✗

3 I can talk about what's around me.  ✓ ? ✗

4 I completed Review 3!  ✓ ? ✗

Goodbye from Rise and Shine Towers

1 Trace. Then write and say.

I can see a ...

book

pencil

flower

door

tree

bird

bag

ball

School

book
_____
_____

_____
_____

Park

_____
_____

2 7.05 Listen and number.

a

b

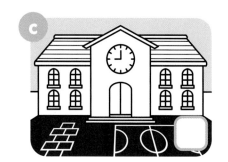
c

3 Trace. Then circle.

It's a school.
I can see books / flowers.

It's a park.
I can see desks / trees.

4 Look and write. Then point, ask and answer.

Is it a/an …?

Yes, it is./
No, it isn't.

~~music box~~
strawberries
elephant
bird   party
rabbit

1 music box

2 _____

3 _____

4 _____

5 _____

6 _____

5 Trace. Then sing the Goodbye song.

Goodbye!
Happy holidays!

It's autumn!

1 🎧 8.04 ✏️ Trace and match. Then listen and colour.

(tree) (leaf) (apple) (chestnut) (pumpkin) (fire)

Winter holidays

2 🎧 8.08 Trace and match. Then listen and number.

(hat) (gloves) (scarf) (boots) (snow) (lights)

Spring is here!

3 🎧 8.12 Trace. Then listen and number.

☐ 1 ☐ ☐ ☐

egg   blossom   chick   lamb   flower   rabbit

Sunny summer days

4 🎧 8.16 Trace. Then listen and circle.

I'm wearing my
(sun hat) / swimming costume.
I'm wearing a sun hat / sunglasses, too.
All ready to play,
On a sunny / picnic, summer day.

I'm wearing my
swimming costume / sunglasses.
We've got a beach / picnic lunch.
Let's have an ice cream each,
And go to the picnic / beach!

Picture Dictionary

Welcome

Vocabulary

 bag   book   chair   desk   door   pencil

Unit 1

Vocabulary 1

 ball   car   doll   elephant

 robot   tablet teddy bear train

Vocabulary 2

 big   new

 old   small

Unit 2

Vocabulary 1

 auntie   brother   dad   grandad

 granny   mum   sister   uncle

Vocabulary 2

 bird   cat

 dog   fish

Unit 3

arms   ears   eyes   feet

hands   legs   mouth   nose

dance   hop

jump   run

Unit 4

bananas   bread   cheese   chicken

milk   olives   strawberries   tomatoes

ice cream   milkshake

pizza   sandwiches

Unit 5

duck   fox   frog   lizard

mouse   owl   rabbit   turtle

ant   bee

butterfly   ladybird

Unit 6

Vocabulary 1

 dress

 jumper

 pyjamas

 shirt

 shoes

 shorts

 trousers

 T-shirt

Vocabulary 2

 cold

 happy

 hot

 sad

Autumn

Vocabulary

 apple

 chestnut

 fire

 leaf

 pumpkin

 tree

Winter

Vocabulary

 boots

 gloves

 hat

 lights

 scarf

 snow

Spring

Vocabulary

 blossom

 chick

 egg

 flower

 lamb

 rabbit

Summer

Vocabulary

 beach

 picnic

 sunglasses

 sun hat

 sunny

 swimming costume